I0901485

Citizenship at School

UNDERSTANDING CITIZENSHIP

Corina Jeffries

CIVICS FOR THE REAL WORLD™

Rosen Classroom™

Citizens are people who belong to a community. Your school is a community. You are a citizen of your school community.

It's important to be a good citizen at your school. It shows you care for yourself and your classmates.

Don't hog the scissors. Be a good citizen by sharing with your classmates. Everyone should have a chance to learn.

Don't talk when someone else is talking. Be a good listener. This shows respect for the person who is talking.

Some students might read books that you don't like. Keep an open mind. Maybe you will learn something new.

If you have a question, raise your hand. Everyone can have a turn to say what they think.

Are you responsible? This means you can be trusted to do what is right. If you make a mess, be responsible and clean it up.

When you cooperate, it means you work nicely with others. Cooperate with your classmates and school will be more fun.

Listen to your classmates' ideas. They might know how to make your science project better.

Be kind, show respect, and work together. It's easy to be a good citizen at school!

WORDS TO KNOW

book

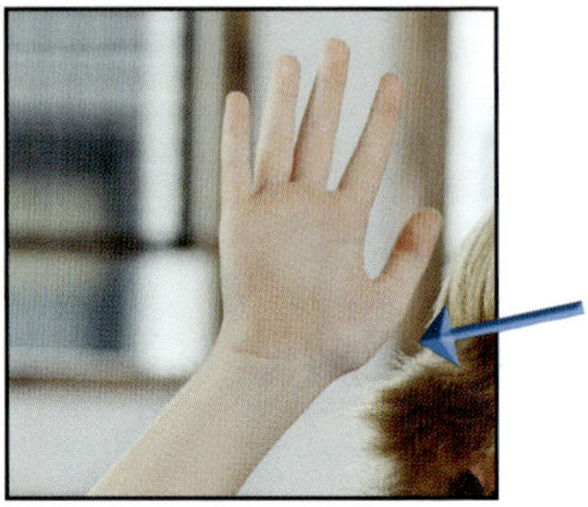

hand

scissors